SHORT WALKS YORKSHIRE DALES

SEDBERGH, KIRKBY LONSDALE AND INGLETON

by Jonathan and Lesley Williams

Looking across to the northern Howgills from the route to Fox's Pulpit (Walk 12)

CONTENTS

Using this guide.. 4
Route summary table 6
Map key 7
Introduction.. 9
   Walking in the Western Dales...................................... 9
   Where to stay.. 10
   Travel 11

The walks
1. Sedbergh and the River Rawthey............................ 13
2. Sedbergh and the River Lune 17
3. Sedbergh and Winder....................................... 23
4. Sedbergh, Millthrop and Farfield Mill 27
5. Cautley Spout 33
6. Uldale and the upper Rawthey.............................. 37
7. Pendragon Castle and Tommy Road 43
8. Wild Boar Fell... 49
9. Dentdale's Coal Road and Arten Gill 55
10. Dent and Green Lane 61
11. Dent to Sedbergh 67
12. The Lune Valley and Fox's Pulpit 73
13. Barbon and Barbondale 79
14. Kirkby Lonsdale and the River Lune 85
15. Ingleton Waterfalls Trail 91

Useful information... 95

USING THIS GUIDE

Routes in this book

In this book you will find a selection of easy or moderate walks suitable for almost everyone, including casual walkers and families with children, or for when you only have a short time to fill. The routes have been carefully chosen to allow you to explore the area and its attractions. Most routes are circular or out-and-back, although some linear walks may be included that use public transport to get back to the start. Although there may be some climbs there is no challenging terrain, but do bear in mind that conditions can sometimes be wet or muddy underfoot. A route summary table is included on page 6 to help you choose the right walk.

Clothing and footwear

You won't need any special equipment to enjoy these walks. The weather in Britain can be changeable, so choose clothing suitable for the season and wear or carry a waterproof jacket. For footwear, comfortable walking boots or trainers with a good grip are best. A small rucksack for drinks, snacks and spare clothing is useful. See www.adventuresmart.uk.

Walk descriptions

At the beginning of each walk you'll find all the information you need:

- start/finish location, with a what3words address to help you find it
- parking and transport information, estimated walking time, total distance and climb
- details of public toilets available along the route and where you can get refreshments
- a summary of the key highlights of the walk and what you might see

Timings given are the time to complete the walk at a reasonable walking pace. Allow extra time for extended stops or if walking with children.

The route is described in clear, easy-to-follow directions, with each waypoint marked on an accompanying map extract. It's a good idea to read the whole of the route instructions before setting out, so that you know what to expect.

Maps, GPX files and what3words

Extracts from the OS® 1:25,000 map accompany each route. GPX files for all the walks in this book are available to download at www.cicerone.co.uk/1248/gpx.

What3words is a free smartphone app which identifies every 3m square of the globe with a unique three-word address, e.g. ///destiny.cafe.sonic. For more information see https://what3words.com/products/what3words-app.

USING THIS GUIDE

Walking with children

Even young children can be surprisingly strong walkers, but every family is different and you may need to adapt the timings given in this book to take that into account. Make sure you go at the pace of the slowest member and choose a walk with an exciting objective in mind, such as a cave, river, waterfall or picnic spot. Many of the walks can be shortened to suit – suggestions are included at the end of the route description.

Dogs

Sheep or cattle may be found grazing on a number of these walks. Keep dogs under control at all times so that they don't scare or disturb livestock or wildlife. Cattle, particularly cows with calves, may very occasionally pose a risk to walkers with dogs. If you ever feel threatened by cattle, you should let go of your dog's lead and let it run free.

Enjoying the countryside responsibly

Enjoy the countryside and treat it with respect to protect our natural environments. Stick to footpaths and take your litter home with you. When driving, slow down on rural roads and park considerately, or better still use public transport. For more details check out www.gov.uk/countryside-code.

The Countryside Code
Respect everyone
- be considerate to those living in, working in and enjoying the countryside
- leave gates and property as you find them
- do not block access to gateways or driveways when parking
- be nice, say hello, share the space
- follow local signs and keep to marked paths unless wider access is available

Protect the environment
- take your litter home – leave no trace of your visit
- do not light fires and only have BBQs where signs say you can
- always keep dogs under control and in sight
- dog poo – bag it and bin it – any public waste bin will do
- care for nature – do not cause damage or disturbance

Enjoy the outdoors
- check your route and local conditions
- plan your adventure – know what to expect and what you can do
- enjoy your visit, have fun, make a memory

ROUTE SUMMARY TABLE

WALK NAME	START POINT	TIME	DISTANCE
1. Sedbergh and the River Rawthey	Sedbergh Info Centre	1hr	3km (1¾ miles)
2. Sedbergh and the River Lune	Sedbergh Info Centre	3hr	10.5km (6½ miles)
3. Sedbergh and Winder	Sedbergh Info Centre	2¼hr	6.5km (4 miles)
4. Sedbergh, Millthrop and Farfield Mill	Sedbergh Info Centre	2¼hr	7.5km (4¾ miles)
5. Cautley Spout	Cross Keys Inn, Cautley	2hr	5.5km (3½ miles)
6. Uldale and the upper Rawthey	Parking near Rawthey Bridge	1¾hr	6km (3¾ miles)
7. Pendragon Castle and Tommy Road	Roadside parking on Tommy Road	2hr	7km (4¼ miles)
8. Wild Boar Fell	Roadside parking at The Thrang	3hr	9.5km (6 miles)
9. Dentdale's Coal Road and Arten Gill	Dent station	2¾hr	10km (6¼ miles)
10. Dent and Green Lane	Dent village centre	2¾hr	8km (5 miles)
11. Dent to Sedbergh	Dent village centre	2½hr	9.5km (6 miles)
12. The Lune Valley and Fox's Pulpit	Lowgill Viaduct	2¾hr	8.5km (5¼ miles)
13. Barbon and Barbondale	Barbon war memorial	2½hr	9km (5½ miles)
14. Kirkby Lonsdale and the River Lune	Kirkby Lonsdale market square	2¼hr	8km (5 miles)
15. Ingleton Waterfalls Trail	Broadwood car park, Ingleton	3hr	7km (4¼ miles)

ROUTE SUMMARY TABLE

HIGHLIGHTS
The town, the school and riverside walking
Western Howgills, riverside walking
Great views from an easy hill above Sedbergh
Old mills, low fells and a welcoming cafe
England's tallest above-ground waterfall and a pub with no beer
A secret valley and gentle waterfalls
Two ancient castles and fine views
A great hill with a flat top
Settle–Carlisle railway, industrial heritage and an immense viaduct
Old moorland tracks, riverside walking and the village
Riverside walk on the Dales Way
Remote Luneside walk and a historic site
Gentle walking above the village
Exploring the old town and the Lune
Waterfalls, waterfalls, and more waterfalls

SYMBOLS USED ON ROUTE MAPS

S Start point

F Finish point

SF Start and finish at the same place

4 → Waypoint

~ Route line

MAPPING IS SHOWN AT A SCALE OF 1:25,000

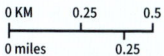

DOWNLOAD THE GPX FILES FOR FREE AT
www.cicerone.co.uk/1248/gpx

Sign pointing across the Rawthey towards Cautley Spout (Walk 5)

INTRODUCTION

The Howgill Fells rise above Sedbergh, seen from the River Rawthey (Walk 4)

The Western Yorkshire Dales provide a fascinating blend of landscape and history. Surrounded by hills, you don't need to climb very high to appreciate the far-reaching views; ridges and moorland ripple into the distance, dissected by deep valleys where neat drystone walls divide an intricate pattern of fields, isolated barns and ancient whitewashed stone farmhouses. Explore the valleys and you will find enchanting market towns and villages with cosy pubs and historic buildings, where cobbled streets lead down to riverside footpaths and beautiful arched stone bridges.

This is a border landscape; to the north lies the Eden Valley and Scotland, with the Lake District to the west, and the Pennines and Yorkshire to the east. Easily accessible, yet relatively quiet and unspoilt, the area has much of interest to delight a visitor, from stunning waterfalls, riverside meadows, wild and empty moorland, to gigantic railway viaducts and fascinating museums that bring the local history to life.

Walking in the Western Dales

The Western Dales provide superb walking. Wide open moors and expansive views make it a mecca for walkers. The small summits and secretive valleys, farms, towns and villages, cafes and pubs provide excellent opportunities for shorter and easier walking, and it is these that are the focus of this guide. All but one of the walks in this guide are circular, most with options to shorten or lengthen if desired. There are occasionally steep hills to climb, but none are especially

Signage near Low Branthwaite (Walk 2)

difficult, although the direct route up Cautley Spout (Walk 5) is steep but can be avoided.

The Western Dales are also the home of a series of long-distance trails with names that resonate for strong hikers – The Dales Way, Dales High Way, Pennine Way, Pennine Journey and Pennine Bridleway all promise excellent walking and are borrowed by many of the routes in this guide.

Many of the hills sit upon limestone, which makes mainly for dry walking, but others rest on sandstone and gritstone (which harbour more vegetation and water), so a number of the walks will have sections that are a bit less dry. It's undoubtedly a rainy area – the lovely green hillsides attest to this – so some walks are best kept for dry days and fine clear visibility.

Many of the walks pass through farms where you will see evidence of the farming life and doubtless meet the warm, welcoming farming communities of these Dales. Keep your dog under close control, ideally on a lead, around any livestock. Dogs will need to be fit – many of the stiles are narrow or awkward, and though many have dog doors not all do. Hay is an important crop so avoid walking through fields that will be or have recently been harvested.

Where to stay

There are many (usually farmhouse) B&Bs throughout the area. The main centres have campsites close by.

Sedbergh, home of the famous school and England's book town, is at the centre of the area. With shops and most facilities, it is a central base for all the routes. Several routes start directly from the town centre and others from nearby.

Dent is a remote village in an adjoining valley but well placed for many of the walks. With pubs, cafes, camping, hotels and B&Bs, and walks direct from the village it has much to offer. Two routes start in the centre of Dent and one from Dent station, a 15min drive away.

Sedbergh's main street (Walks 1–4)

A steam train runs over Arten Gill viaduct on the Settle–Carlisle rail line (Walk 9)

Kirkby Lonsdale is at the southern extent of the area, a busy small market town with all facilities and many spots to eat, although fewer walks directly from the town. A single route starts here and one from nearby Barbon, but it's a good base.

Slightly outside the area, **Kirkby Stephen** and **Hawes** have plenty of accommodation, campsites, shops and places to eat but are a short drive from Sedbergh and Dent.

Likewise, **Ingleton** on the edge of the area and close to Ingleborough and the Three Peaks, has a range of camping, B&B, shops and restaurants. The Waterfall Walk (Walk 15) starts here.

Travel

From the north and south, the M6 provides the best road access, with the A65 and A66 the main east/west arteries. Trains come to Oxenholme, and from there it is a short taxi or bus ride into the Dales. Or take the Settle–Carlisle railway for a scenic approach, with stops at Ribblehead, Dent, Garsdale and Kirkby Stephen on the edge of the area covered in this guide.

All walks in this guide can be reached by car, with good parking in the main centres. Other walks may use limited roadside parking – park considerately, off the road and not blocking any entrances. Take extra care if driving in late May and early June when the Appleby Horse Fair takes place; the distinctive ponies and travelling carts fill the roads and sometimes the parking spaces as well.

There are limited buses in the area, mainly run by the volunteer Western Dales service. Any relevant bus services are mentioned in the information box of each walk. Details of websites and routes are given in the 'Useful Information' appendix.

The Pepperpot, renovated in 2015

WALK 1
Sedbergh and the River Rawthey

Start/finish	*Sedbergh Information Centre*
Locate	*///ignites.doses.allows*
Cafes/pubs	*Plenty in Sedbergh*
Transport	*Buses S5 and 563 from Kendal, 54 from Kirkby Stephen, S1 from Dent*
Parking	*Joss Lane car park (LA10 5AD) and Loftus Hill (LA10 5RX)*
Toilets	*Sedbergh, near the start on Main Street*

Time 1hr
Distance 3km (1¾ miles)
Climb 60m

A gentle riverside walk, a curious folly, and a return through the grounds of Sedbergh School

This short walk includes a brief riverside walk with a return through the grounds of Sedbergh School and town, passing by the curious folly known as the Pepperpot. There's an option to extend the walk from the hamlet of Birks across level fields to visit the historic Quaker meeting house at Brigflatts, built in 1674.

The tourist information centre in Sedbergh

SHORT WALKS YORKSHIRE DALES

1 Turn left at the tourist information centre. Cross over the **A683** onto Vicarage Lane beside playing fields. Continue ahead, rising to cross a driveway to reach a junction of paths. Turn right, descending across a meadow to a squeeze stile onto a road. Walk down the road and just before the bridge take the footpath on the right (to the right of a driveway) signed to Birks.

2 Cross a meadow and enter woods, following signs for the Dales Way. Emerge into a sloping field with **the Pepperpot** seen on the top of the hill just to the left.

Dating from 1910, this former summerhouse was built by Charles Edward Taylor, a local chemist, who owned nearby Akay house and estate. The estate and summerhouse were abandoned after WW2. In 1948 a curious cow wandered in and climbed the stairs to enjoy the view – it took five men with ropes to coax her down!

3 After exploring the Pepperpot, continue on the path down between trees to walk beside the River Rawthey on the left edge of playing fields – keep dogs under close control. A large white building, Birks House, is seen ahead. Climb steeply and briefly to a path junction in front of **Birks House**.

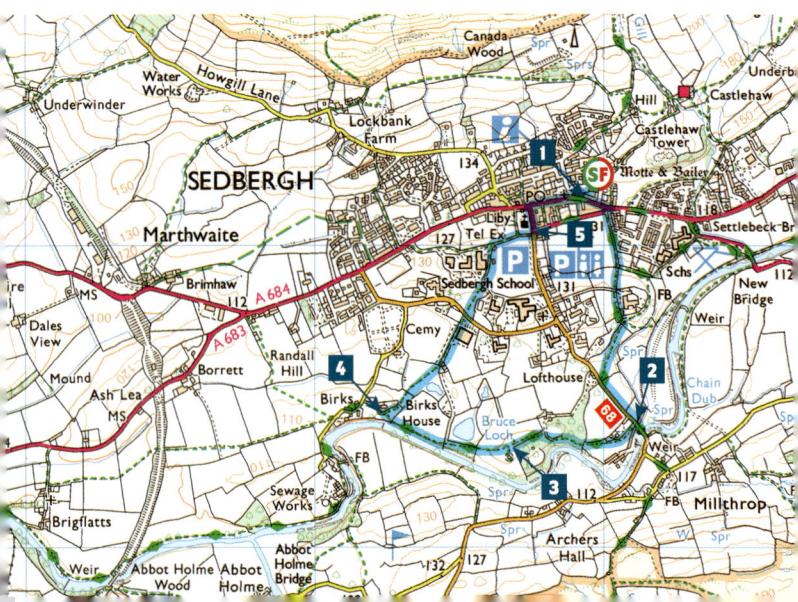

Passing old cottages in Birks

4 Turn right here and follow the path above the playing fields, then continue, now on a track with the Hurst Centre on the right. Cross straight over a road and up on the signed footpath, keeping the **Sedbergh School** buildings on your left and playing fields on the right. Turn right at the second path

Low water in the Rawthey

junction beside the cricket ground, then pass the parish church on your left to meet the road opposite the school library. The building currently housing Sedbergh School library was once the old grammar school, dated 1716.

5 Turn left, then turn right to walk along Main Street and back to the information centre.

> ### + To lengthen
> To visit the Quaker meeting house at Brigflatts, from Waypoint 4 continue straight, turn left onto the road through Birks, then right after the last house on a path directly across fields signed to Brigflatts, emerging opposite the Quaker burial ground. The meeting house is just to the left (see Walk 11 for more information). Return the same way to Birks. Adds 2km (30min).

Sedbergh School

Sedbergh School was founded in 1525 (so celebrating 500 years in 2025) by Cambridge scholar Thomas Lupton, who was born at Cautley. At first it occupied the building now used as the school library by the Loftus Hill car park. The school is renowned for its sporting prowess, the annual Wilson Run (a punishing 10-mile cross-country run), the school Song 'Winder' and a wide range of distinguished alumni. The school first admitted girls in 2001 and now has around 600 pupils aged 13 to 18 years old, as well as a thriving junior school located in Casterton.

Sedbergh School library

WALK 2
Sedbergh and the River Lune

Time 3hr
Distance 10.5km (6½ miles)
Climb 200m

Explore the quiet west of the Howgills, returning to Sedbergh along the rivers Lune and Rawthey

Start/finish	Sedbergh Information Centre
Locate	///ignites.doses.allows
Cafes/pubs	Plenty in Sedbergh
Transport	Buses S5 and 563 from Kendal, 54 from Kirkby Stephen, S1 from Dent
Parking	Joss Lane car park (LA10 5AD) and Loftus Hill (LA10 5RX)
Toilets	Sedbergh, near the start on Main Street

This longish walk starts with a gentle climb out of Sedbergh to the west of the Howgills on a small lane, before a riverside walk first beside the Lune then the Rawthey brings you back into Sedbergh along the Dales Way. The route takes a good half day with plenty to enjoy. It's easy walking but there are no facilities along the way. It is just as good in reverse, going out along the Dales Way and returning down Howgill Lane.

Lincoln's Inn Bridge

The wide Lune Valley seen from the walk towards Height of Winder

1 Head west down Main Street then turn right immediately after the Dalesman Country Inn up **Howgill Lane**. Pass the People's Hall and the last houses and climb steadily, with widening views north and south along the Lune Valley. Pass a turn on the right that heads onto the fells and then turn left after 150m to **Height of Winder Farm**.

2 Turn left into a field, then right around the farmhouse and enter a large field, following the path down to the bottom corner. Carefully cross a small road (listen for traffic) and continue down the next field, keeping just left of a barn. Keep heading down and at a T-junction continue towards Low Branthwaite. Cross a stream and turn left before **Low Branthwaite Farm** onto the Dales Way.

3 Follow the grassy path, aiming for a prominent signpost at the top of the field to approach the **Lune Viaduct**, an impressive sight.

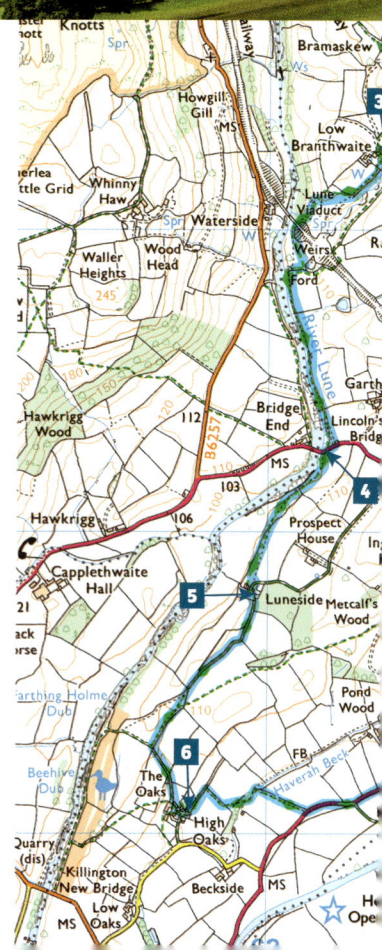

WALK 2 – SEDBERGH AND THE RIVER LUNE

The Ingleton branch line ran from Clapham to Sedbergh and rejoined the main line at Lowgill before Tebay. Largely closed in 1954, its abandoned viaducts, like the Lune Viaduct, testify to how well it was built.

Pass under the vast pillars and continue to a bridge and a stile. Follow the path through fields, with the attractive **River Lune** alongside behind trees, to meet the A684 road at **Lincoln's Inn Bridge**.

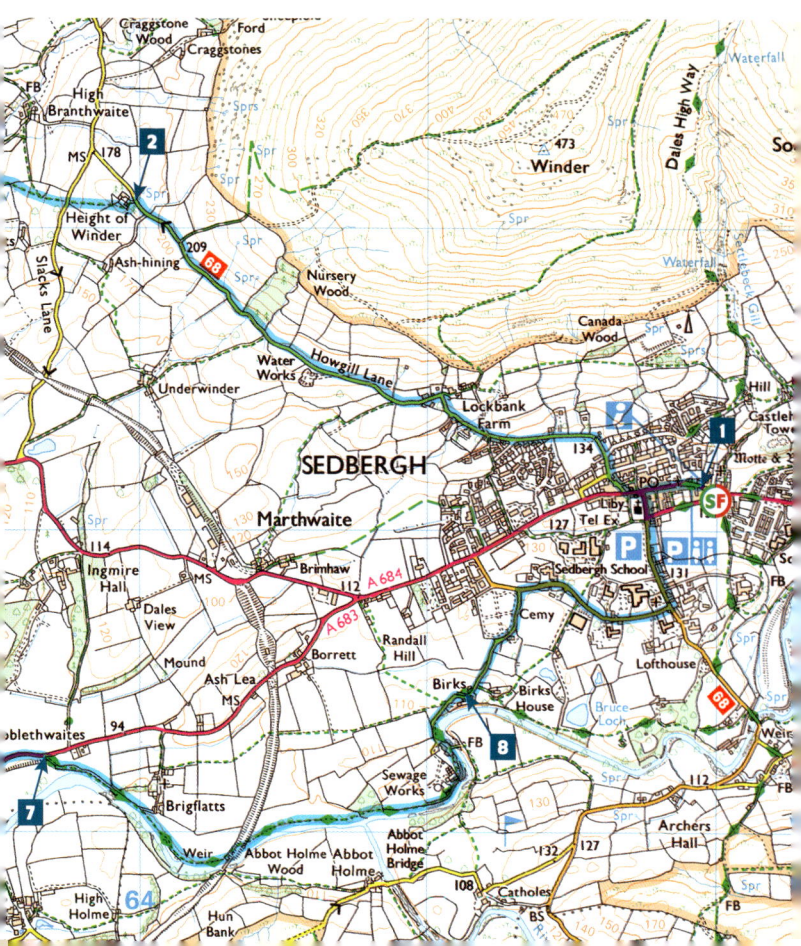

The impressive Lune Viaduct

The name suggests a connection with the renowned Inn of Court in London, but the source is unclear. Records suggest that the bridge dates from the 17th century is made of 'mixed random rubble' – but it looks much stronger than this suggests.

4 Carefully cross the busy road by the bridge and descend a small stile into fields, with open views south alongside the river. Helpful informal signs made by the farmer at Luneside Farm steer you away from the river, through a stile, alongside a field and past the farm 10min from the bridge.

5 Continue along a lane, at first enclosed by hedges and then follow the Dales Way, keeping to the top (left edge) of a large meadow. Turn left along a lane and into the hamlet of **The Oaks**. Turn right here to enter Killington Bridge Local Nature Reserve on the banks of the Lune, returning to The Oaks on the same route, a detour of about 15min.

6 Turn left to leave the hamlet and then right and between hedges before crossing an open field. Cross a stone bridge and field to reach the A683 road. Turn left along the verge. After 10min find a right turn signed 'Birks Mill 1¼ miles'.

WALK 2 – SEDBERGH AND THE RIVER LUNE

7 Follow the path, initially narrow, between a fence and the River Rawthey, which here is only slightly smaller than the Lune that will soon subsume it. Pass close by the **Briggflatts** Quaker Meeting House. There is no access to the meeting house from this path. Continue through fields, pass over the old railway line for the last time, then past the confluence of the Rawthey and Dee rivers (the Dee coming from Dent), and continue through fields leading onto a lane rising up to **Birks**.

8 Pass an old mill, now used by a foodservice business, then turn up a narrow lane past the cottages at Birks to reach a junction with a larger road. Turn right, passing playing fields and buildings of **Sedbergh School**, then left at the T-junction beside a chapel, now heading towards the town centre. Turn right into Main Street and back to the start.

> ⓘ *Several rivers flow through the area; all drain towards Lancaster and Morecambe Bay except the River Eden, which flows north to Carlisle and the Solway Firth.*

The placid River Lune below Lincoln's Inn Bridge

The path descends above the ravine of Settlebeck Gill

WALK 3
Sedbergh and Winder

Start/finish	*Sedbergh Information Centre*
Locate	*///ignites.doses.allows*
Cafes/pubs	*Plenty in Sedbergh*
Transport	*Buses S5 and 563 from Kendal, 54 from Kirkby Stephen, S1 from Dent*
Parking	*Joss Lane car park (LA10 5AD) and Loftus Hill (LA10 5RX)*
Toilets	*Sedbergh, near the start on Main Street*

Time 2¼hr
Distance 6.5km (4 miles)
Climb 420m

With dramatic views over Sedbergh, this is a short, sometimes steep fell walk, mainly on grass with some rough and stony sections

A climb out of Sedbergh to the summit of Winder, the first summit on the Howgills, gives access to the southern part of the range and a quick descent back into town. It's easy walking, if steep, with commanding views over the area covered in this guide. Extending the route to Higher Winder gives some more fine, high walking.

Joss Lane signage marks the route back into town

1 From the tourist information centre go west along Main Street and turn right by the public toilets. Head up Joss Lane and follow the road as it bends right by the Farfield clothing outlet. Go through a gate and into fields, passing above houses to the right. After the first narrow stile continue along a path by the ravine gouged by **Settlebeck Gill** and go through a metal gate out onto the open fell, which looms above with a welcome bench close by.

WALK 3 – SEDBERGH AND WINDER

2 Turn left above the wall that separates the open access fellside from the farmland below and continue on a good path until you pass the gates into **Lockbank Farm**. It's possible to shorten the route at this point by dropping down through the farm and following the road back into Sedbergh.

3 Follow the wall as it slants uphill. After about 300m (10min) follow the path as it bears right away from the wall and continue in a fairly straight line along the grassy and occasionally unclear path. After around 1hr from the start (1km from Lockbank Farm) come to a broad grassy path climbing the fell.

4 Turn right and climb steadily, with broadening views west to the Lake District and along the Lune Valley, to reach the summit of **Winder**.

> By tradition, all Sedbergh School pupils need to climb Winder at least once during their time at the school. Probably many climb it much more than that – it's an ideal spot for getting perspective on the town and region generally.

5 Continue past the summit along a wide path of trodden grass, heading steadily downhill. Come to a broad ridge with the hillside sloping away on each side. Just under 20min from Winder, and just as the path begins to

Looking down over Sedbergh and the hills beyond

Looking ahead to Arant Haw

> ⓘ In 2006 Sedbergh became England's only book town. Other book towns include Hay-on-Wye (Wales) and Wigtown (Scotland).

climb up Arant Haw (often called Higher Winder), find a grassy path to the right heading directly down the hill.

6 Turn right on this and follow the path as it levels out and continues above the rather dramatic slopes into **Settlebeck Gill**, following the route (marked on the map but not the ground) of the Dales High Way. Various routes cross the hillside, but stay on the lower path, crossing a rocky section just before the end of the fell, which could be awkward if it is snowy or icy. Continue through the stile and alongside the ravine carrying the gill, then follow the paths and roads climbed at the start and back down Joss Lane into **Sedbergh**.

− To shorten

After walking along the wall at the bottom of the fell, return to Sedbergh by turning left through Lockbank Farm then along Howgill Lane, giving a walk of 1hr.

+ To lengthen

At Waypoint 6, before turning down to Settlebeck Gill, continue up to Arant Haw (Higher Winder) and return, an extra 2km (30min).

WALK 4
Sedbergh, Millthrop and Farfield Mill

Start/finish	*Sedbergh Information Centre*
Locate	*///ignites.doses.allows*
Cafes/pubs	*Pubs and cafes in Sedbergh, cafe at Farfield Mill*
Transport	*Buses S5 and 563 from Kendal, 54 from Kirkby Stephen, S1 from Dent*
Parking	*Joss Lane car park (LA10 5AD) or Loftus Hill (LA10 5RX)*
Toilets	*Sedbergh, near the start on Main Street, and Farfield Mill*

This walk visits two former mill sites via a clear fell path, with some intricate navigation through farmland, and gives fine views of the Howgills. Take in the renovated Farfield Mill and cafe, followed by a riverside walk back to Sedbergh. Most of the stiles are narrow, there may be a few boggy bits after wet weather and there are several roads to cross, so take care and keep dogs under close control.

Time 2¼hr
Distance 7.5km (4¾ miles)
Climb 200m

Howgill views en route to Farfield Mill craft centre and cafe, with a mainly level scenic walk beside the River Rawthey back to Sedbergh

Springtime bluebells in the riverside woods

SHORT WALKS YORKSHIRE DALES

1 Turn left down the narrow Main Street, cross Back Lane and head down Vicarage Lane past the entrance to Winder House. There are excellent views back to the Howgills over the town. Just after a rise take a path heading right through a stile and cross a sloping field. Take care through a narrow stile onto a road and turn left downhill then over the old bridge across the **River Rawthey**. Continue for 40m to the right, then turn left up the narrow road into **Millthrop**.

Millthrop is the site of an old mill – dating back to the 14th century and redeveloped during the 1790s

Old cottages in the hamlet of Millthrop

WALK 4 – SEDBERGH, MILLTHROP AND FARFIELD MILL

– which produced horse blankets. The tiny weavers' cottages are now prized houses in a picturesque hamlet.

2 Turn right through the hamlet, passing the cottages, and as you near the end find a track on the left signed to Frostrow Fell. Head uphill through gates into open farmland. After 10min come to a wall and turn left onto a grassy path signed to High Side. You are soon on a broad ridge with fine views north to the Howgills above Sedbergh, and a stream below to the right. Keep on the ridge path for about 20min, then when the path appears to fork, find a narrow path heading downhill, slightly right, leading towards a crossing point over **Clatter Beck**, then keep left beside a wall rather than right up Frostrow. Go through a small gate and past a house, **Highside**, then head downhill on the

Looking over Sedbergh to the Howgills from the broad ridge above Millthrop

The River Rawthey

track. Just as it becomes a paved road at a sharp left-hand bend, turn right over a stile and down a very steep field, then make a short climb to a road by **High Hollins Farm**.

3 Go right for 10m and follow signs through the farm. Go through gates and drop down a steep track. Just after a stream, turn right and follow the stream to a stile in the upper right corner of the field. Cross this, then another field and stile. Keep on, drop down to another stile, cross a small steam and climb to a narrow stile that opens onto a fast road, so take care. Go left along the road for 30m then turn right through another narrow stile. After two fields come to **Farfield Mill**.

4 Continue past the mill and follow a narrow lane to reach the main road by **Straight Bridge**. The bridge may be straight but the road is not.

5 Cross and immediately turn left through yet another narrow stile and follow the path alongside the Rawthey. This becomes narrow and occasionally uneven with tree roots as you approach Sedbergh and emerge onto a road at **Settlebeck Bridge**.

> ⓘ *The Dent fault is a major fault separating the carboniferous limestone of the Yorkshire Dales from the older rocks of the Howgill fells. Check out the Sedgwick Geological Trail: www.cbdc.org.uk/CumbriaLGS/Leaflets/8_001.pdf*

WALK 4 – SEDBERGH, MILLTHROP AND FARFIELD MILL

6 Cross the road and take the path that continues along the riverside, here wider and more open. Keep right and then right again and climb a field to come to the rise passed on the way out of Sedbergh. Descend and take Vicarage Lane into town and back to the information centre in **Sedbergh**.

> **– To shorten**
>
> It's about a 45min walk from Sedbergh to Farfield Mill alongside the river (reversing the route described). Return the same way, giving a round trip of 1hr 30min.

Farfield Mill

The mill was built in 1837 and operated into the 1970s as a blanket maker. It is now a craft centre with an excellent cafe and shop. There are exhibitions telling the story of the lives of the weavers, and some of the old looms and water/steam machinery to see. The crafts on display and for sale in the shop include weaving, painting, pottery, jewellery making and others. The cafe is on the bottom level, by the river.

Buildings at Farfield, the scene of busy industry for several centuries

Approaching the falls on a good path

WALK 5
Cautley Spout

Start/finish	*Near Cross Keys Inn at Cautley*
Locate	*///entrust.caressing.cleanser*
Cafes/pubs	*Temperance inn at Cautley*
Transport	*Infrequent bus (563) to Cross Keys, occasional bus from Sedbergh to Cautley*
Parking	*Roadside near the Cross Keys (LA10 5NE)*
Toilets	*No public toilets on route*

Time 2hr
Distance 5.5km (3½ miles)
Climb 330m

A steep climb to England's tallest waterfall, with picnic spots along the way

The climb up Cautley Spout is short and on a good path, but it is steep and airy. If it looks as though your head for heights will be challenged, or if walking with young children, turn back or ascend via the return route. It's a walk that is best done in fine weather, after it's been raining for a day or more, to get the best of the waterfalls. In winter ice can accumulate on the upper part of the route.

The good path up valley towards the spout

1 From the roadside parking, drop down across a sturdy footbridge over the **River Rawthey** and follow the good path as it climbs in steps into the substantial valley, with emerging views of the Spout. This valley was the site of an iron-age farming settlement, and there is evidence of crops being grown as well as sheep and cattle farming.

2 As the path begins to climb in earnest after 30min, decide whether you think it's too steep for you to get up and down. Paths head left and right but the main route is clear and climbs grassy slopes by **Cautley Spout** before coming to a steep stone staircase. Climb this alongside the waterfalls all the way to the top after the second stream crossing.

> **The series of cascades of Cautley Spout are England's tallest above-ground waterfall extending over nearly 200m. The falls drain a substantial part of the Howgill Fells, so there is always some water, and they sometimes freeze in winter when climbers will come to test themselves on the ice.**

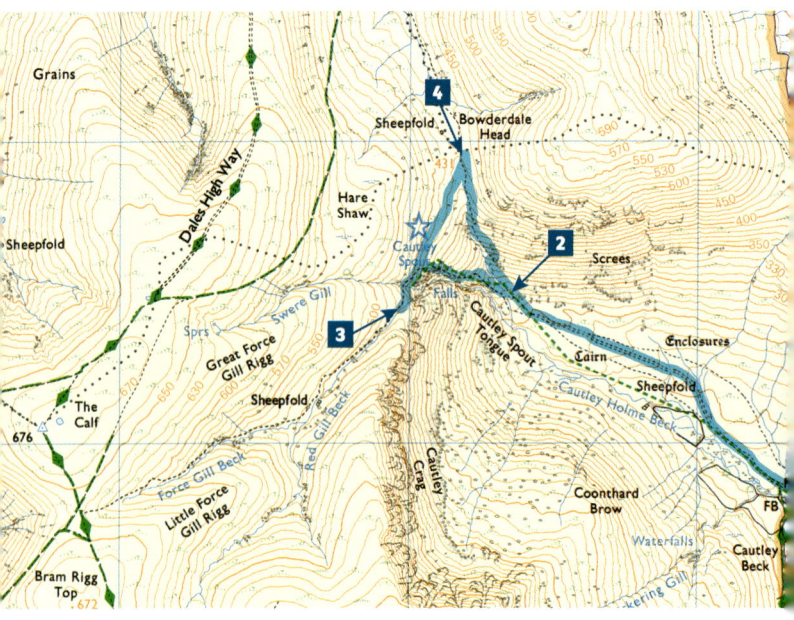

WALK 5 – CAUTLEY SPOUT

3 When you are ready to descend, reverse the last section of the climb and find a narrow path headed across the grassy hillside about 5min down, just where the main path starts to drop steeply. Take this and follow it for about 400m (10–15min) until it meets a path at **Bowderdale Head** that runs from Cautley into the long valley of Bowderdale, unseen to your left.

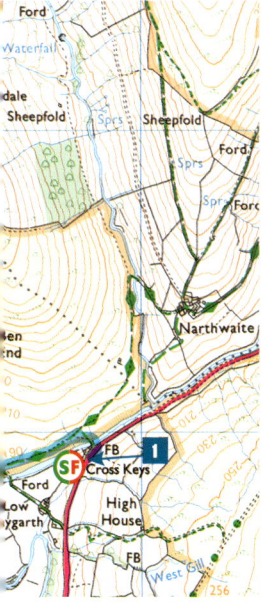

The upper section of the waterfall

4 Turn right and follow the path down through zigzags then more easily down to meet the path used to climb the Spout. Turn left and follow this down through the valley and back to the road.

Looking back down the valley with Baugh Fell in the background

− To shorten
Turn back if you feel it's going to be too steep or try the descent route in reverse.

+ To lengthen
From the top of the falls follow the small path alongside the attractive Force Gill Beck, passing an old sheepfold and heading slightly right to reach the highest point in the Howgills, Calf, at 676m. Return the same way and rejoin the main route. Out and back to Calf adds 3.75km (1hr 30min).

The Cross Keys – a pub with no beer!

The Cross Keys Inn is a temperance inn – it serves no alcohol but does offer good food and other refreshments. It was donated to the National Trust in 1949 on condition that it remained a temperance site. The building dates back 400 years and has been an inn for over 300, with strong Quaker connections over the period that continue up to today.

WALK 6
Uldale and the upper Rawthey

Time 1¾hr
Distance 6km (3¾ miles)
Climb 200m

An easy walk exploring a secret valley surrounded by wild hills and waterfalls

Start/finish	Roadside parking west of Rawthey Bridge
Locate	///doped.clips.proposals
Cafes/pubs	None on route
Transport	No public transport
Parking	Three parking areas near Rawthey Bridge (CA17 4LN)
Toilets	No public toilets on route

A secret valley hidden among some of the highest hills in the area, waterfalls, picnic spots and swimming pools make this a memorable walk. There are no dramatic moments or cafes, but the quiet satisfaction of exploring a hidden valley. Pick good weather, preferably after a dry spell, as the approach can be a little damp underfoot, and take a picnic, making a day of this short excursion to Uldale.

The route crosses fields and farms as it returns to the valley

1 From the parking cross the road and head left, then before **Rawthey Bridge** take a track dropping down on the right. Pass through the gate and follow the public access track, formerly the Bluecaster Road. After 15min (600m from the road) reach the first signpost.

2 Turn left at the signpost. The path runs along the foot of the vast Baugh Fell into Uldale and can be a bit boggy after rainfall. Continue along the undulating path, with fine views of the expanse of Wild Boar Fell and Swarf Fell ahead as well as the line of farms across the valley that you will pass on the return walk. After 50min (3km) from the start come to a bridge over the infant River Rawthey.

3 Here the route can be extended by continuing ahead to a series of modest waterfalls. To continue the main route, cross the bridge and climb in the woods. About halfway up a small sign directs you left. Follow this path down across a stream and come

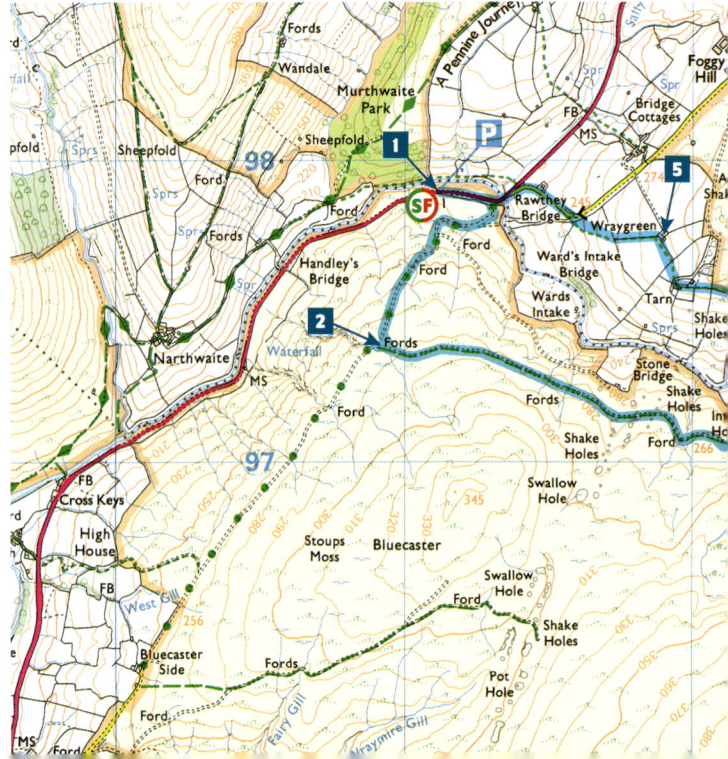

WALK 6 – ULDALE AND THE UPPER RAWTHEY

Needle House

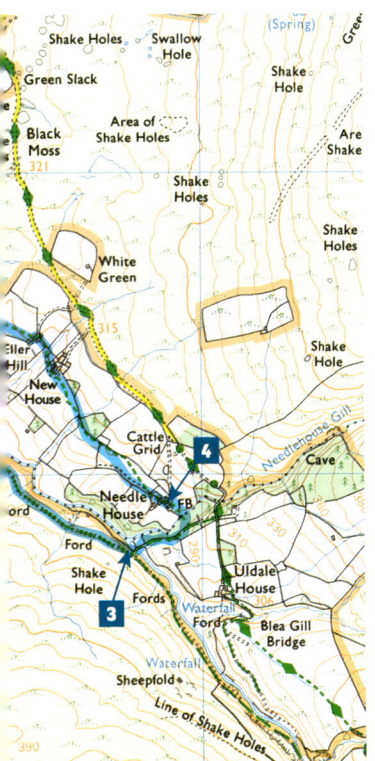

to the impressive buildings of **Needle House**.

4 Pass between the surprisingly large buildings and continue through fields for the return trip. Keep to the

The Rawthey is a small stream in its upper reaches

Wild Boar Fell and Swarth Fell rise high above Uldale

> ⓘ *Dales farming terms:*
> ***Outrake** – enclosed track between walls*
> ***Intake** – fields above the old medieval fields on lower fells*
> ***Garth** – enclosed space*
> ***Thwaite** – clearing*

right in the first large field, go through a wooded gap and pass the white buildings of **New House**. Pass between disused buildings and cross more fields to enter some open access moorland on a path which could be rather damp underfoot. Keep above the reeds. Go between the buildings of the outdoor centre at **Tarn** to reach **Wraygreen**.

5 Follow the field wall downhill and after the gate strike out diagonally right across the field. Come out on a road and follow this to the main A683. Turn left over the bridge, taking extra care as the traffic is fast just here, and return to the start point.

✚ To lengthen

Continue upstream from the bridge over the Rawthey near Needle House (Waypoint 3), passing waterfalls, picnic spots and possible swimming spots (a 45–60min round trip). You could also start the walk from the Cross Keys Inn, adding 4km and 1hr 30min to the route.

Rough Fell sheep

Rough Fell sheep are one of the three hefted breeds native to Cumbria and are mainly found around Kendal and Sedbergh. They have black faces with a distinctive white nose, and are friendly, extremely hardy and long lived. Their wool is prized for making carpets, while the meat is renowned for its flavour.

Pendragon Castle

WALK 7
Pendragon Castle and Tommy Road

Start/finish	*On Tommy Road near the railway tunnel*
Locate	*///monkey.mistress.searching*
Cafes/pubs	*None on route*
Transport	*No public transport*
Parking	*Informal parking on the verge on Tommy Lane (CA17 4JX), close to spot height 318m on the map*
Toilets	*No public toilets on route*

Time 2hr
Distance 7km (4¼ miles)
Climb 200m

Two castles, two ancient monuments – easy walking on an old lane and tracks across moorland

The broad Upper Eden Valley, also known as Mallerstang, leads south from Kirkby Stephen. Its entrance is guarded by several castles, the best of which is Pendragon Castle. Before dropping to the river and the castles, the walk explores a section of moorland from a lane, Tommy Road. This brief encounter with the Upper Eden needs a car as there is no public transport and there are no facilities on route.

Views over the Mallerstang Valley from Tommy Road

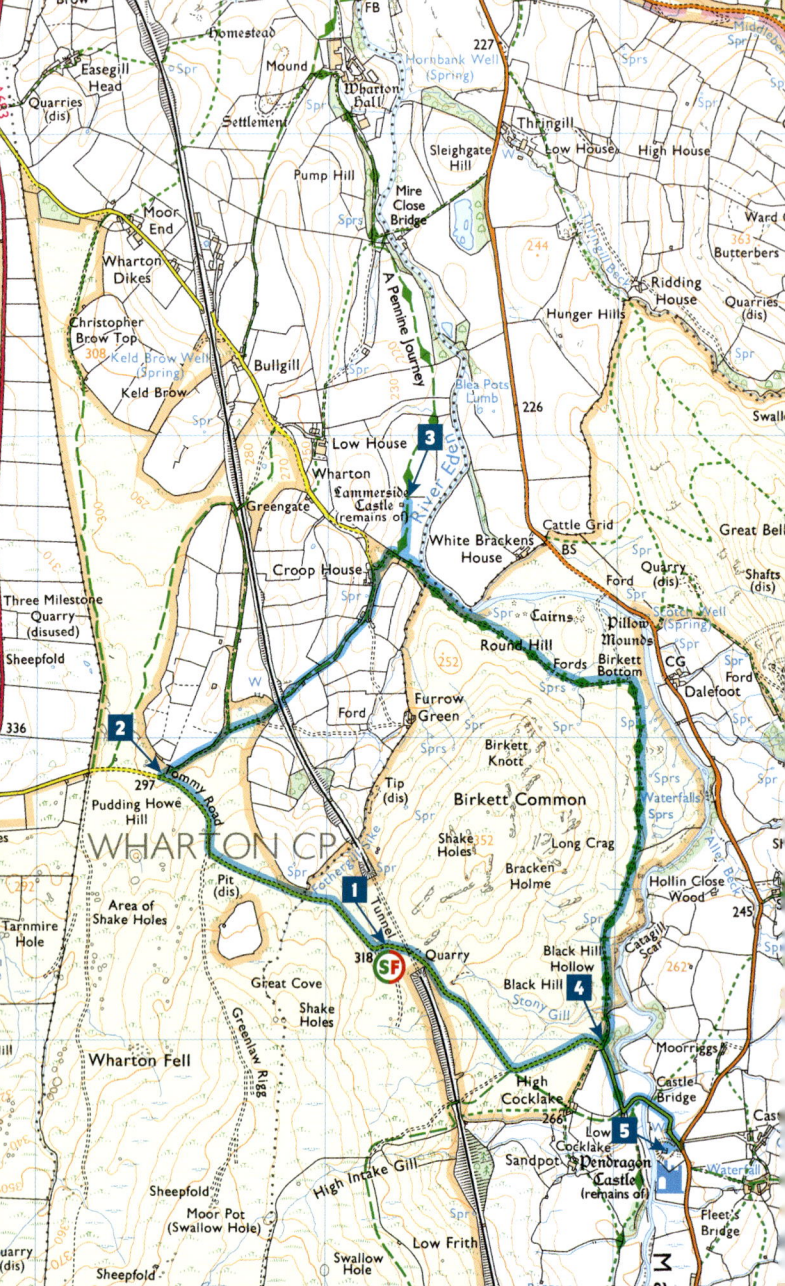

WALK 7 – PENDRAGON CASTLE AND TOMMY ROAD

The ruined remains of Lammerside Castle

1 Head up the road, which is very quiet – you may see no cars at all – and after 10min pass a high point where there are more parking options. Views open up across to the Howgills. Drop down by the road and as it bottoms out find a turn right signed to Croop House along the lane called **Tommy Road**. Sadly the origins of the name seem to be lost – you made a great route, Tommy!

2 Turn right and after 5min bear right at an unmarked junction of wide grassy paths. Pass under the Settle–Carlisle railway, now released from its short tunnel. Continue down on a track between walls and keep left as you join a road that leads to the farm buildings of **Croop House**. Turn right in front of the farmhouse and head downhill. At a gate turn into a field and inspect the remains of **Lammerside Castle**.

> Lammerside Castle was built in the 12th century for defence against Scots raiders. A tower was added in the 14th century, but it was abandoned in the 17th century as the family moved to Wharton Hall, some 1.5km north towards Kirkby Stephen.

3 Having explored the castle, return to the path and turn left along a byway, a generally good track that soon meets the **River Eden**. Follow the byway or divert across the pasture to follow the river.

The upper Eden

On the left alongside the Eden – close to the bend in the river – are two easy-to-miss scheduled monuments. First there are three Bronze Age burial mounds, and a little further along on the slopes of Round Hill are four pillow mounds, the remains of a medieval rabbit farm known as the Giants Graves.

Continue along the byway, passing a well-preserved lime kiln, and climb slightly to reach Tommy Road.

> ⓘ *Lady Ann Clifford (born 1590) inherited the family estate comprising lands and castles of Brough, Brougham, Appleby, Pendragon and Skipton following decades of legal battles.*

4 Turn left (away from your car) and follow the road downhill round bends, then cross the river and come to the ruins of **Pendragon Castle** on the right.

5 To return to the start point, turn left from the castle entrance and walk up the quiet road back to your parking spot. If you have extra energy, a 10–15min walk up Birkett Common is recommended for the views over the Eden Valley.

> **– To shorten**
>
> Walk down to Pendragon Castle from your chosen parking spot and return the same way, giving a walk of 3km (about 1hr).
>
> **+ To lengthen**
>
> Continue north at Lammerside Castle (Waypoint 3) to see Wharton Hall (not open for visitors). This adds 3km (and an extra 45min) for the round trip.

Pendragon Castle

According to legend, King Arthur's father, Uther Pendragon, built the castle to defend against the encroaching Anglo-Saxons. Local stories tell of his difficulties diverting the Eden to fill his moat, and his death and that of his men when the Saxons poisoned the well. Sadly, there is no remaining evidence of any occupation before the 12th century, as the site was damaged by Scots raiders. Later, it was repaired by Lady Anne Clifford in the 17th century. Pendragon Castle was her favourite of the five castles in her estate. The Lady Anne Way walk follows a route between Skipton and Penrith that this redoubtable Elizabethan lady took between her many castles.

The summit of Wild Boar Fell looms high above the ascent route

WALK 8
Wild Boar Fell

Time 3hr
Distance 9.5km (6 miles)
Climb 450m

The highest fell in the region above Mallerstang and one of the best walks, but no boars anymore!

Start/finish	*Roadside parking at The Thrang*
Locate	*///uplifting.roadmap.february*
Cafes/pubs	*None on route*
Transport	*No public transport*
Parking	*Roadside at The Thrang (CA17 4JX), with other limited possibilities close by*
Toilets	*No public toilets on route*

Wild Boar Fell is one of the highest hills in the area and makes for an excellent walk, especially in fine weather, with wonderful views towards Ingleborough, the Lakes, Howgills, Eden Valley and Pennines. Parts of the climb are steep, but the summit area is flat and the good path is generally dry. The best views are from The Nab. Avoid this walk in poor visibility, as there is a steep drop to the east and the flat summit is difficult to navigate in cloud.

Looking back to Hazelgill farm at the start of the climb

Looking ahead to Wild Boar Fell from the start point

1 From the small parking area at The Thrang, cross the road and take a track leading to Deep Gill Farm. After 3min, turn left across grassy fields with only a trace of a path to **Hazelgill Farm**. In case of doubt walk to this point along the valley road.

2 Cross the driveway and go through a gate to find the continuing path. Keep to the left of the house up the sloping path. Pass under the Settle–Carlisle railway; soon the path makes a hairpin turn right. Follow it beside a wall behind abandoned buildings and cross a stream to enter the open fellside.

The route is shared with the Pennine Bridleway

WALK 8 – WILD BOAR FELL

3 Climb steadily. Pass new tree planting on your right and follow the modest marker posts through the area of Angerholme Pots and reach the wall at **High Dolphinsty**. The Nab looms above like a mini-Matterhorn; happily, it's much easier to reach.

4 Turn left by the wall (the continuing path drops towards Ravenstonedale) and climb the steepest part of the route, known as Scriddles Ridge, and 1hr 30min from the start reach the excellent viewpoint at **The Nab**.

> ⓘ *Shakeholes and potholes marked on the map in this area may lead to underground caves. Take care.*

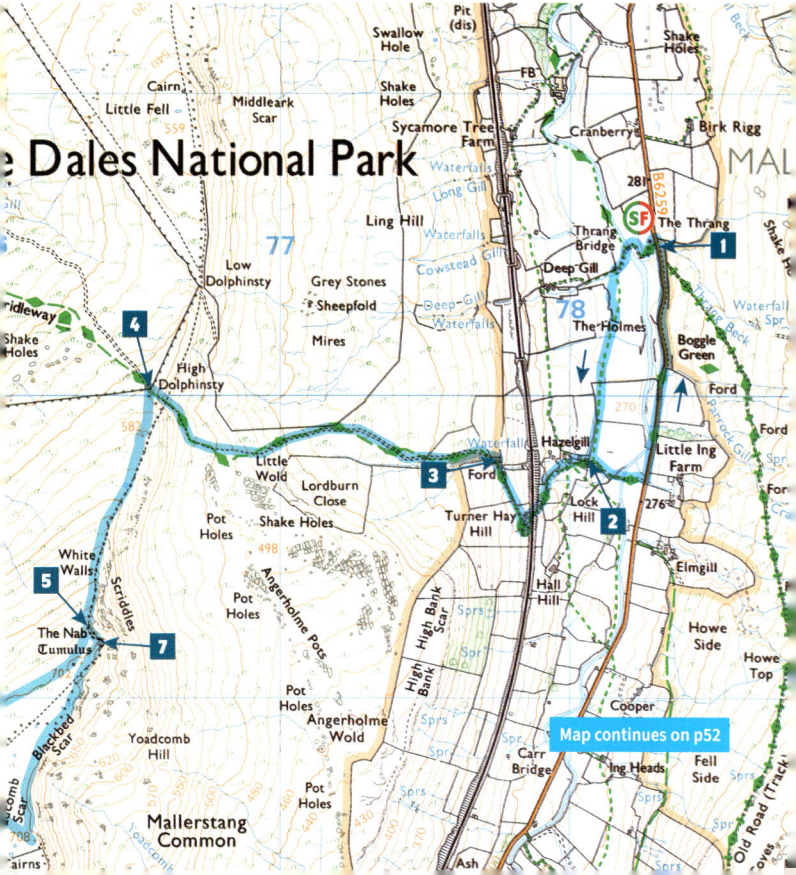

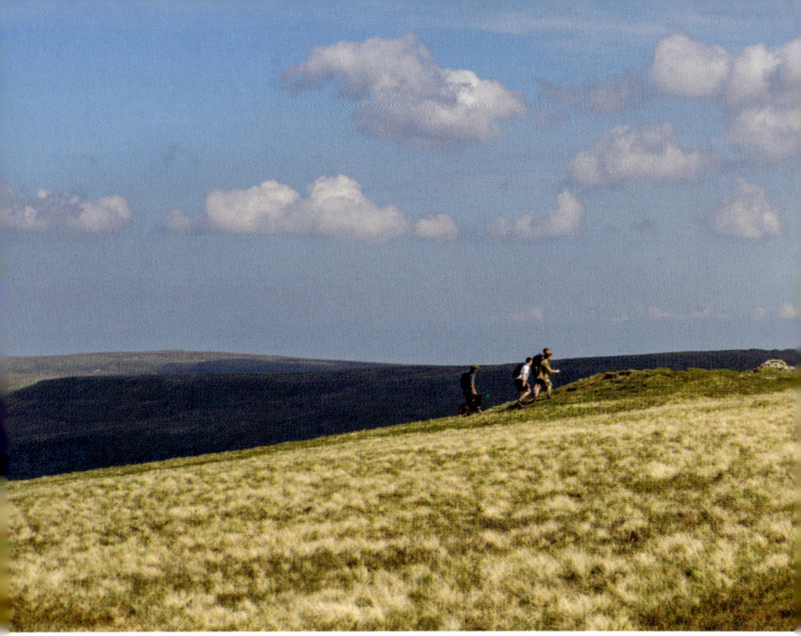

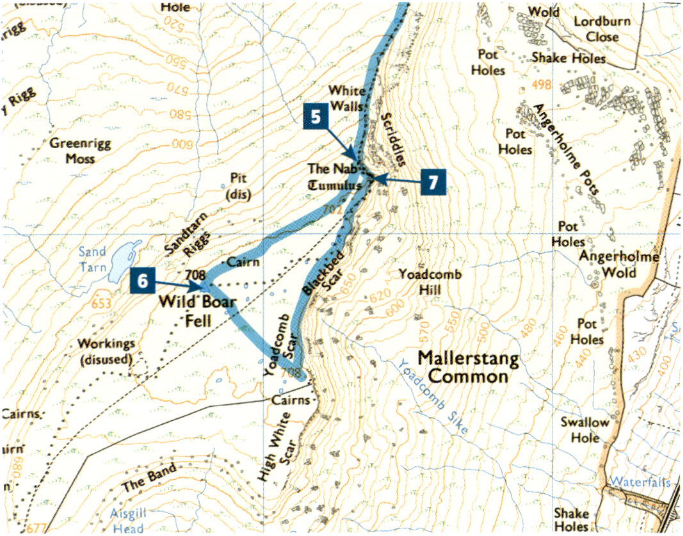
Hole
Greenrigg Moss
Pit (dis)
White Walls
5
The Nab
Tumulus
7
Scriddles
Sandtarn Riggs
Sand Tarn
Cairn
708
6
Wild Boar Fell
Workings (disused)
Blackbed Scar
Yoadcomb Scar
Yoadcomb Hill
Mallerstang Common
Yoadcomb Sike
Cairns
High White Scar
The Band
Aisgill Head
Wold
Lordburn Close
Pot Holes
Shake Holes
Angerholme Pots
Angerholme Wold
Swallow Hole
Waterfalls

Walkers reaching the summit plateau

5 Continue across to the cairn at the summit of **Wild Boar Fell**.

At 708m, Wild Boar Fell is the fifth highest peak in the Yorkshire Dales. Unsurprisingly the name is believed to come from the boar who roamed the slopes of the hill. A tusk, claimed to be from the last boar, is in Kirkby Stephen parish church.

6 The trip directly out and back to The Nab takes about 20min. For a loop adding an additional 15min, head sharply left (south-east) from the summit of Wild Boar Fell to the interesting area called **Yoadcomb Scar**. From a distance Yoadcomb Scar looks like a series of monuments, although up close it's a few solid cairns, the origin of which is not known. Continue north close to the edge of the scar back to The Nab.

7 To return, retrace your route to High Dolphinsty, descend to **Hazelgill Farm** and continue to the valley road, following signs for the Pennine Bridleway. Turn left along the road and back to the parking which is 10min further.

> **— To shorten**
> Turn back at The Nab, cutting the route by 2km (30min).

Walking on the grassy track with the flat top of Ingleborough in the background

WALK 9
Dentdale's Coal Road and Arten Gill

Start/finish	Dent station
Locate	///taskbar.voice.care
Cafes/pubs	Pub near Cowgill (check opening times)
Transport	Train to Dent on Settle–Carlisle rail line
Parking	Car park at Dent station (LA10 5RF), very limited parking at Waypoints 2 and 4
Toilets	No public toilets on route

Time 2¾hr
Distance 10km (6¼ miles)
Climb 350m

Fine views from one of England's highest roads, a steep but rewarding climb and the Settle–Carlisle rail line

Combining one of England's highest roads, the renowned Coal Road, a moorland track and hints of the area's industrial heritage, this walk captures the very best of the Western Dales and upper Dentdale. There are vast views, so aim for clear weather, and wrap up warm if it's windy – the moorland track is almost level but without protection from the elements. The route can be done in either direction; it depends on whether you prefer to climb steeply on the road or up Arten Gill.

Dent station, the highest in England

SHORT WALKS YORKSHIRE DALES

1 Look over the station before setting off – it gives a hint of life in the Victorian age. Turn right out of the station, cross a bridge over the line and head uphill on the **Coal Road**, with forestry on the left and open moorland to the right. After 30min and just before the road starts to drop down, turn right on a broad track. There are a couple of parking spots here.

Looking down the Coal Road to Great Coum above Dentdale and Barbondale

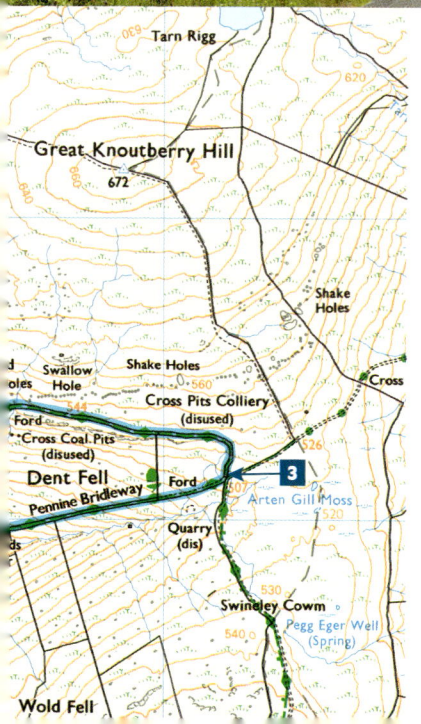

The Coal Road connects Dentdale and Garsdale over a 535m (1750ft) pass and is named for the surface coal workings on Great Knoutberry Hill passed on the route ahead.

2 Follow the excellent track used by the Pennine Bridleway. It is well constructed and is usually dry as it skirts under **Great Knoutberry Hill** and far above the Settle–Carlisle line and the upper reaches of Dentdale. There are views across to Deepdale and back down Dentdale, while ahead Whernside and Ingleborough dominate the view. After about 45min, or just under 3km along the track, pass the old coal workings at **Cross Pits**, now overgrown, and drop down to a four-way junction.

3 Turn right, still following the Pennine Bridleway. The wide path descends steadily down **Arten Gill**, then under the immense Arten Gill Viaduct.

The viaduct was constructed in the 1870s to carry the Settle–Carlisle railway line. Partly built from Dent marble, a form of black limestone, it dominates the valley. It's an awesome sight; the trains, some steam driven, pass high above, evoking the height of the railway boom.

Arten Gill Viaduct is impressively big

Continue down past houses and a bridge over the River Dee.

4 Turn right down the road, passing the Sportsman's Inn (the only refreshments en route) after 5min. Continue along the quiet road where you are likely to meet more Dales Way walkers than cars. Cross the bridge at **Lea Yeat** and turn right. The hamlet of Cowgill is just beyond the turn.

5 Signs announce the steep hill (17%) and warn of winter snows. Climb steeply taking care on the twisty road under trees before reaching open fell.

In Cowgill, before starting the steep climb back to Dent Station

Continue the climb, which stays steep, but maybe a little less steep than at the bottom, to reach the **station**.

> **− To shorten**
>
> Retrace your steps from any point along the track under Great Knoutberry for a walk that is likely to take no more than 2hr. Alternatively, park at Waypoint 2 and walk out and back along the high, almost level track.

Settle–Carlisle Railway

This most rural of England's railways was built in the 1870s. It shows examples of some of the country's best railway construction, including tunnels and famous viaducts such as at Ribblehead and Arten Gill. Dent is England's highest station; the station building has been redeveloped with a B&B and parking.

The line escaped the 'Beeching cuts' of the 1960s but was scheduled for closure in the 1980s. A strenuous campaign rescued the line from oblivion, and it now carries over 1.2 million passengers per year as well as freight. Steam trains run on many days, giving a real feel for what rail travel must have been like 150 years ago.

The start of the Nun's House Outrake path

WALK 10
Dent and Green Lane

Time 2¾hr
Distance 8km (5 miles)
Climb 300m

A high route above the Dent Valley with great views of the Western Dales

Start/finish	Dent village centre
Locate	///pheasants.crowned.rang
Cafes/pubs	Pubs and cafes in Dent
Transport	Irregular S1 bus Wednesday and Saturday, plus Friday in summer
Parking	Car park in Dent (LA10 5QL)
Toilets	In Dent at the car park

An interesting and varied walk above the Dent Valley on an old byway, Green Lane – known locally as the Occupation Road or 'Occy' – with great views of the surrounding Dales. There is a steep start alongside a gill in a ravine, a high-level traverse of the fellside and a gentle walk back by the river. Some of the higher paths and tracks get a bit rough and stony but this doesn't impact on this great tour of Dentdale.

Dent parish church

1 Head uphill on the road named 'Dragon Croft' directly opposite the car park (although signs are few and far between). The road goes between houses and passes the Meditation Centre before twisting right then left and becoming a track that climbs steeply alongside a ravine – Flinter Gill. The path is steep and stony but makes good progress so hang in there. Pass a barn to the right and come out into open countryside, and after 1.4km or around 40min (depending on how fast you climbed the path) come to the junction with **Green Lane**. This is also known as the Occupation Road or 'Occy', a name resonating from the 18th-century enclosures of shared open land.

2 Turn left along the lane. It's mainly a good track, often grassy, sometimes stony, but with a few rutted and soggy sections as in times past it saw motorbike traffic but is steadily recovering. After another 40min come to a well-signed junction, the high point of the route at 415m.

> This section has splendid views across the Dent Valley to Aye Gill Pike, back to the Howgills above Sedbergh, and ahead to Great Knoutberry and Whernside. You are among the best of the Western Dales.

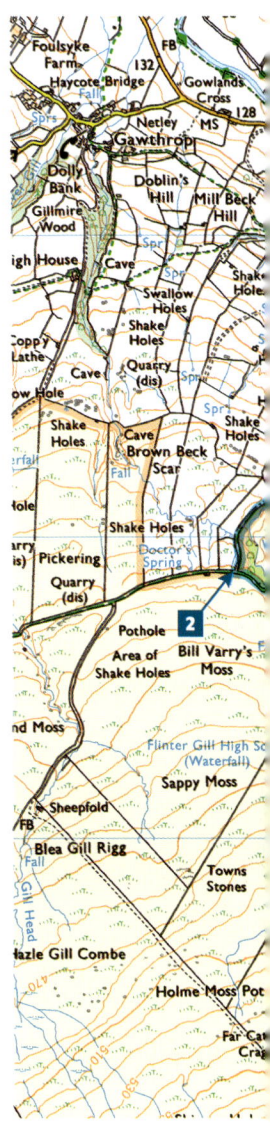

WALK 10 – DENT AND GREEN LANE

63

The gate at the top of Flinter Gill climb as the path joins the 'Occy'

3 Turn left. The path down **Nun House Outrake** is shared with the local sheep and can be a little muddy and gets stonier as you descend. Pass a small farm building and come to a narrow road by **Peacock Hill Farm**.

4 Continue down past the farm through two gates and into fields to reach the disused building at **Scow**. Swing left and pass through three gates to find a small path near a yellow sign on an electricity pole and drop into woods above Deepdale Beck. Cross the road near **Mill Bridge** and take a path between fields and the beck. An alternative route is to continue along the road at Peacock Hill Farm and descend before the farm at Slack on paths (overgrown in summer) to Mill Bridge.

At this point the paths carrying the Dales Way, the Dales High Way and the Pennine Journey routes all combine to head towards Dent, passing the confluence with the River Dee.

5 Follow paths alongside the river. You will see Dent getting closer to your left. The path swings left away from the river, through a gate, then right to reach a road at **Church Bridge**. Turn left before the bridge and walk into Dent; either wander through the churchyard or explore the cobbled streets before returning to the start point. Pubs are in the centre of the village and cafes a little further on near the car park.

WALK 10 – DENT AND GREEN LANE

> ### – To shorten
> At Waypoint 4 at the bottom of the Nun House Outrake by Peacock Hill Farm, turn left along the road and return directly to Dent, saving 1km and 15min. Or retrace your steps to Dent when you reach Green Lane, which gives a 2.8km (1hr) walk.

The Terrible Knitters of Dent

The knitters of Dent were actually 'terribly' good! The poet Robert Southey published an article in 1834 describing the women of Dent, who would knit while walking to and from work in the fields, and in the evenings would gather to continue knitting and tell stories. They used double tipped needles, making hats, jackets, gloves and waistcoats from a thick greasy yarn called 'bump', as well as items from a softer yarn; these were then sold to provide a valuable second income.

Church Bridge marks the final turn into Dent

Several solid bridges cross streams beside the River Dee

WALK 11
Dent to Sedbergh

Start	Dent village centre
Finish	Sedbergh
Locate	///metro.unwound.senders
Cafes/pubs	Pubs and cafes in Dent and Sedbergh
Transport	Irregular S1 bus Wednesday and Saturday, plus Friday in summer
Parking	Car parks in Dent (LA10 5QL) and Sedbergh (LA10 5AD)
Toilets	At car park entrance in both Dent and Sedbergh

Time 2½hr
Distance 9.5km (6 miles)
Climb 140m

Along the Dales Way beside the River Dee, finishing with a moorland trail with views of the Howgills and Sedbergh

A mostly level walk on grassy paths beside the River Dee, with a short easy climb through woods and open hillside with interesting views throughout. The route follows the Dales Way, so navigation is easy. In spring the fields and hillsides are filled with flowers, lambs scamper and play and the riverside is alive with birdsong. The route involves numerous gates, stiles and occasional uneven and muddy sections. It is also possible to do this as a circular walk returning to Dent by shortening the route from Waypoint 3.

The Sun Inn, Dent

SHORT WALKS YORKSHIRE DALES

1 Begin opposite the George and Dragon in the centre of Dent. Take the left fork with the large Sedgwick memorial stone water fountain on the left, go past the church and down the hill with a small shop on the right. Continue towards **Church Bridge**, but as you start onto the bridge find a path signed 'Hippens' on the left.

> The Sedgwick water fountain is dedicated to Dent-born Adam Sedgwick (1785–1873), a founder of modern geology, who discovered the Dent Fault. A Cambridge mathematician, his interest in geology culminated in his becoming president of the Geological Society and a Fellow of the Royal Society.

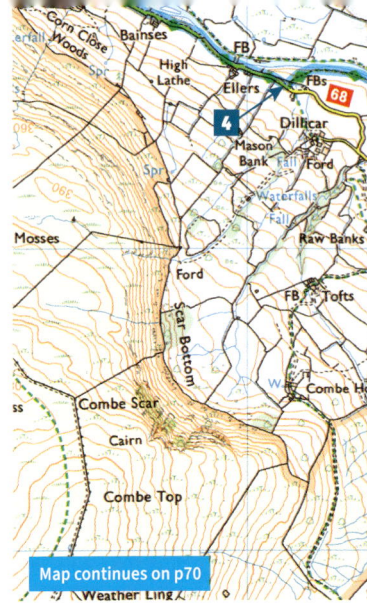

Sedgwick memorial stone in Dent

2 Drop onto the riverside path and join the **Dales Way** with fields and views of Dent village to the left, passing through four fields to reach the valley road. Turn right then almost immediately right again to continue on the riverside path. Climb steps and cross the valley road at **Barth Bridge** through a squeeze stile.

> The Dales Way is a 127km (79 mile) long-distance route through the Western Dales from Ilkley to the Lake District, finishing at Bowness-on-Windermere. It's an ideal first multi-day walking route – passing through pretty Dales villages including Grassington, Hawes, Dent and Sedbergh.

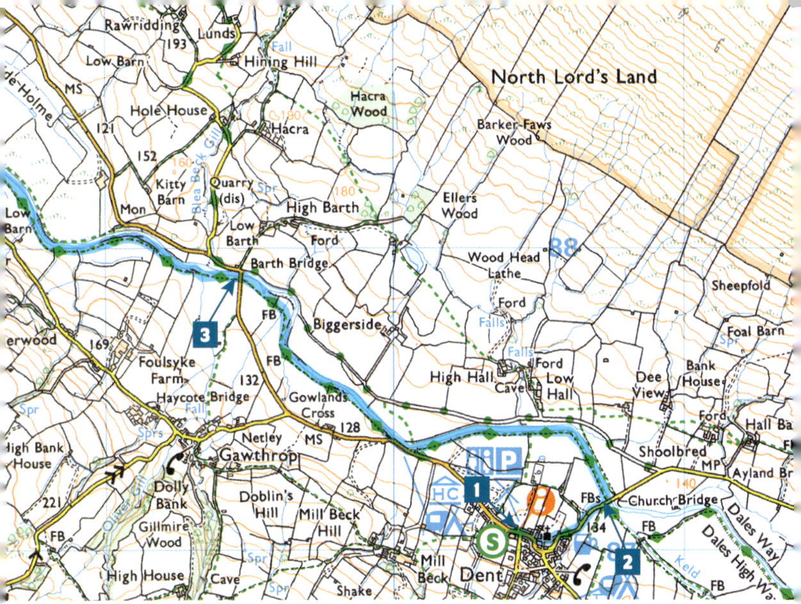

Looking back to Dent early in the walk alongside the River Dee

WALK 11 – DENT TO SEDBERGH

3 Squeeze through another stile to continue beside the river. After about 25min turn away from the river at a sign just before the end of a field beside a minor road. This leads to a footbridge over a stream and onto a minor road. If you miss the sign you will run out of path and need to retrace your steps!

4 Turn right along the minor road and follow this for about 25min, when you will reach the cluster of farm buildings at **Brackensgill**. Take the path to the right, cross two footbridges then head up the track to the main valley road.

5 Cross straight over the road and walk up the track between ancient high stone walls, forking left at a junction. At a farm continue straight ahead across a field, then enter woods, still climbing. Leave the woods and continue between stone walls leading to a high grassy area with views of the Howgills directly ahead and Sedbergh below. The path descends directly towards Sedbergh. Pass through a gate and down an enclosed stony track to reach the hamlet of **Millthrop**.

6 Turn right, passing pretty stone cottages, then turn left to the main

The first view of Sedbergh and the Howgills before the descent through Millthrop

After Rawthey Bridge the route ascends gradually into Sedbergh

road. Turn right, cross the bridge over the **River Rawthey** and after 2min take the signed path right across fields then over a rise with a large school building on the right. Descend directly ahead to reach the A684 (Back Lane). Cross over into Main Street and the centre of **Sedbergh**.

▬ To shorten

At Waypoint 3 turn right over the road bridge and immediately right onto a minor road (Hall Lane). Follow this for about 30min all the way back to join the road near Church Bridge just below Dent village. Turn right and return to the start. Saves 5km (1hr 30min).

Farming in the Dent Valley

Farming in the Dent Valley is mainly focused on sheep and cattle. Each farm has land stretching from the flat river valley meadows, predominantly grazed by cattle, up through the steep valley slopes onto high rough pastures ideal for tough Rough Fell and Swaledale sheep grazing. You can see this traditional pattern of fields separated by drystone walls extends up into the higher slopes of the surrounding hills.

WALK 12
The Lune Valley and Fox's Pulpit

Start/finish	Lowgill Viaduct
Locate	///blanking.lemons.shepherdess
Cafes/pubs	None on route
Transport	No public transport
Parking	Near viaduct at start of route (LA8 0BL)
Toilets	No public toilets on route

Time 2¾hr
Distance 8.5km (5¼ miles)
Climb 300m

The banks of the Lune and a famous site in the evolution of the Quaker movement in the shadow of the Howgills

A remote walk starting by a superb viaduct, taking in an ancient bridge, some of the Lune's best riverside walking, fields and farms, and a sharp climb to reach Fox's Pulpit on Firbank, the scene of an important event in the development of the Quakers. As there are no facilities on route, make sure you take sufficient food and water. Good for agile dogs, with a couple of tricky stiles and plenty of doggie swimming possibilities, but as there are likely to be sheep and cattle in the fields, keep dogs on leads.

Fox's Pulpit rocks

Crook of Lune Bridge

1 For the first two sections of the route, you are headed south on the Dales Way. Take the narrow lane under the viaduct and follow it down to a hamlet above the River Lune. Pass **Pool House**, dating from the 1750s. Come to an ancient and narrow bridge across the river – **Crook of Lune Bridge**. Follow the road for 100m uphill and take the footpath directly ahead.

> This beautiful 16th-century bridge is very narrow and an interesting challenge for drivers. The more famous Crook O'Lune bridge painted by JMW Turner is over 30km further south near Caton outside Lancaster.

2 Head south on the grassy track, which drops down alongside the river, passes through woods and fields, and crosses tributary streams. At one point it climbs a bank and becomes narrow for a few metres before dropping down again to sheep-cropped riverside fields. After the second footbridge, keep to the river side of the fence as the path sweeps right and at the end of the field follow the path as it heads away from the river. Just before **Hole House** turn right (off the Dales Way) back towards the river to a good bridge.

3 Cross the bridge and walk directly uphill on a steep and somewhat indistinct path. After 10min reach a road (the B6257) by houses – marked **Goodies** on the map.

4 Go left for 5m and find a continuing bridleway up a lane, through fields and then a lane again. The path slopes left and passes a wood on the left with new planting to the right. Cross into open fields and come to a road. Turn left and reach **Fox's Pulpit** on the left in around 5min. Fox's Pulpit is an isolated rock from which Quaker founder George Fox preached. You can climb up it, with care!

75

5 Retrace your steps along the road and continue straight ahead. There are wide views of the Howgill fells to the right, Whinfell directly ahead, and soon, the Lake District on the left. Pass the Westmorland Motor Club – a Sunday event here may break the peace of this tranquil walk. After 20min, as the road makes a left turn, take a descending path to the right, currently marked by a sign at a jaunty angle.

6 Head down the first field with a wall on the left. Then cross into a second field and continue, now with the wall to the right. Cross three slightly awkward stiles over walls (a good challenge for a dog). Come to a track, wall and pens above **High House Farm**, turn right and descend a field. Initially there are no markings, but the bridleway becomes clearer and eventually becomes a track that loops down to reach the B6257 road.

7 Cross the road and go through a tunnel under the disused railway line. Turn right through a gate before reaching **Davy Bank Farm** and follow the grassy path as it descends. Go through a gate and turn left through the hamlet and up the hill to **Lowgill Viaduct**.

> **– To shorten**
>
> At Waypoint 4 turn right on reaching the B6257 road and follow it back to Lowgill Viaduct, saving 2km (45min).

The viaduct at Lowgill

The Howgills dominate the view as you head north from the pulpit

George Fox and the Quakers

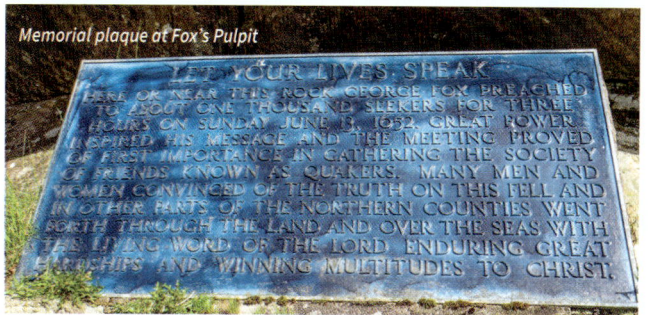

Memorial plaque at Fox's Pulpit

In 1652 George Fox, the founder of the Quaker movement, had a vision on Lancashire's Pendle Hill. Shortly after, he arrived in Sedbergh and preached for three hours at Fox's Pulpit to a gathering of around 1000 'Seekers', amidst the turmoil and uncertainty of the post-civil-war period. The area between Sedbergh, Kendal and Preston Patrick is still known as 'the 1652 country'. An impressive 77-panel Quaker Tapestry illustrates 350 years of Quaker history and is displayed in the Kendal meeting house. After years of persecution, the movement became an important worldwide thread of Christianity.

The memorial cross in Barbon marks the start of the walk

WALK 13
Barbon and Barbondale

Time 2½hr
Distance 9km (5½ miles)
Climb 160m

Explore beautiful Barbondale, with cascades, quiet roads, woods and meadows

Start/finish	War memorial next to the Barbon Inn
Locate	///documents.including.soaks
Cafes/pubs	Pub in Barbon
Transport	No public transport
Parking	Village hall car park (LA6 2LS) and on street – keep driveways clear
Toilets	No public toilets on route

A woodland walk up Barbondale on a broad path with gentle gradients leads to the popular picnic spot at Blindbeck Bridge. Follow a quiet road either directly back to Barbon or via a level road then through meadows. The route could be split into two shorter circular walks. A few tricky stiles through the meadows might cause difficulty for dogs, which should be kept under close control past grazing sheep and cattle.

Barbondale sheep pen

SHORT WALKS YORKSHIRE DALES

1 Begin at the war memorial cross in the village centre and walk past the Barbon Inn, then turn left immediately after the church. Climb on the private road for 500m (12min) through two bends, then at the third bend take the broad path ahead. The black-and-white barrier on the second bend is to protect vehicles and pedestrians during the annual Barbon Hill Climb, held every year.

WALK 13 – BARBON AND BARBONDALE

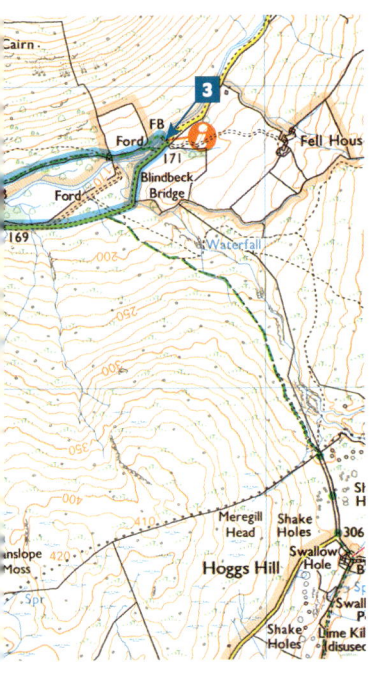

2 Follow the broad path through the woods, keeping just above Barbondale's pretty Barbon Beck, to arrive at a ford over the beck and cross over the wooden footbridge.

Dogs should be kept on leads through High Park, which is a wood and pasture restoration reserve. Enjoy this beautiful spot, which is especially popular for picnics and paddling among the small cascades of the beck.

3 Now turn right, cross **Blindbeck Bridge** and walk along the single-track road, with broad open views, passing an unusual round sheep pen on the right, then at the top of the rise come to a road junction. *The road is usually very quiet, except on sunny weekends.*

The bridge across the Barbon Beck in Barbondale

4 Turn left and enjoy a level walk below **Barbon Low Fell**, with expansive views across the Lune Valley. Pass a cattle grid and continue down past two houses, then at a third house turn right onto a signed footpath.

5 Follow the grassy track across three fields. At the fourth, larger, field head across, tending slightly right near two larger trees to a stile. Cross the driveway for **Whelprigg** then, maintaining roughly the same direction, go through a large field, eventually heading for a gate in the far left corner. Go through the gate onto a lane which bends left to **Low Bank House** farmyard. Keep right of the farmyard through a gate and cross diagonally down to a hidden gate in the lower corner of the field, leading to another field and a minor road.

> ⓘ *On 1 August 2016 the Yorkshire Dales National Park was extended to cover Barbondale and the fells between Dentdale and the Lune valley above Kirkby Lonsdale.*

Fields towards the Whelprigg driveway, on the approach to Barbon

WALK 13 – BARBON AND BARBONDALE

The inn at Barbon

6 Turn right along the road. Just after Underfell Farm, turn left along a bridleway to drop into **Barbon** near the village hall. Turn right to reach the war memorial, with the Barbon Inn close by.

> This small, picturesque village lies at the foot of Barbon Low Fell and features a 17th-century coaching inn and the parish church of St Bartholomew. The Barbon Manor Speed Hill Climb for cars runs twice a year, during June and July – the record is 20.08secs for the 672m.

▬ To shorten

At Waypoint 4 continue ahead along the road, turn left just before the steep hill, then immediately turn right onto a bridleway (before Underfell Farm), to arrive back in Barbon in 20min. This saves 3km (40min).

Wildflowers by the Lune

WALK 14
Kirkby Lonsdale and the River Lune

Start/finish	Kirkby Lonsdale market square
Locate	///terminology.skims.cools
Cafes/pubs	Plenty in Kirkby Lonsdale
Transport	567 bus from Kendal, 581 from Settle
Parking	Several car parks in town but limited to 2hr. Free unlimited parking at Devils Bridge (LA6 2DA)
Toilets	In Jingling Lane and at Devil's Bridge

This is a lovely walk to the south of Kirkby Lonsdale, visiting the historic arched Devil's Bridge and heading along the riverside with views to the east and south. The route passes through the pretty village of Whittington before climbing to a high point near the hamlet of High Biggins, returning to explore Kirkby Lonsdale.

Time 2¼hr
Distance 8km (5 miles)
Climb 120m

Devil's Bridge, a riverside walk, a pretty village and the old market town of Kirkby Lonsdale

Market square, Kirkby Lonsdale

Gentle walking alongside the River Lune

1 From the market square, walk down Jingling Lane then right onto an enclosed footpath. Turn left and immediately before **Devil's Bridge** go through a gap in the wall on the right, keeping to the left edge of the meadow to reach the A65 and cross straight over.

> Devil's Bridge was built during the 13th century, with three graceful arches spanning the River Lune. Legend suggests the bridge was built by the Devil, who left the impression of a hand in a stone at the apex of the bridge.

2 Keeping next to the river, follow the signed path through several kissing gates and stiles, with views ahead to the distant Forest of Bowland. After about 40min cross a long meadow then go up through a further kissing gate then a stile where there is a simple bench seat. The river is teeming with wildlife and in addition to ducks and swans, you may see geese and herons.

3 Turn right onto the path away from the river, keeping to the right side of the field, and head towards **Whittington**. Pass through a gate with a farm on the left, then continue to a road. Turn left, then fork right, rising past houses to reach **St Michael's Church**.

> St Michael's Church at Whittington stands on the site of a former castle, with extensive views. Built in 1875, the oldest part is the tower which is early 16th century.

St Michael's Church in Whittington

4 Now go uphill. Take the narrow lane on the right, immediately opposite the steps to the church. As the lane rises, enjoy the emerging views, with the flat summit of Ingleborough in the distance. On reaching a road go straight ahead for 5min, then continue ahead (left) into **High Biggins**. (Take care: although this is not a busy road, there is no pavement.)

5 Turn right at the T-junction, then where the road bends right, go through a gate to the left down through woods and across a meadow to **Low Biggins**. Turn left, then cross straight over the A65.

6 Pass between school buildings, then down Mitchelgate, lined with traditional stone cottages. Turn right, but before returning to the market square, turn left beside the Sun Inn and walk around the churchyard of St Mary's 12th-century church.

At the far corner of the churchyard are steep steps down to the river (the Radical Steps) and a small Georgian gazebo with views. Just beyond is Ruskin's View, so named when, in 1875, John Ruskin declared it to be 'one of the loveliest views in England, therefore in the world'.

WALK 14 – KIRKBY LONSDALE AND THE RIVER LUNE

> **+ To lengthen**
>
> From Waypoint 3, continue along the riverside path for a further 15min to a fisherman's hut then turn right up Burrow Mill Lane. The lane is usually quite muddy! Turn right through Whittington, then left onto a path 30m after the village hall to St Michael's Church to rejoin the main route. Adds 1.4km (20min) to the time.

Kirkby Lonsdale

Kirkby Lonsdale is a historic market town located at a strategic river crossing on the border of Cumbria, Lancashire and North Yorkshire. The main town centre comprises traditional stone buildings – mainly Georgian, but some much older. Many of the lanes and squares are testament to the history of the town, including Salt Pie Lane, Horse Market, Swine Market and Mitchelgate. St Mary's Church dates from the early 12th century, with huge carved Norman columns, and stained-glass windows. The Victorian art critic John Ruskin, JM Barry of *Peter Pan* fame and the painter JMW Turner were also inspired by Kirkby Lonsdale. The town is especially busy when the popular weekly market is held on Thursdays.

Ruskin's View

Multiple cascades above the falls, with Twistleton Scar above

WALK 15
Ingleton Waterfalls Trail

Start/finish	*Broadwood car park, Ingleton*
Locate	*///salon.initial.extension*
Cafes/pubs	*Cafe at Broadwood car park, pubs and cafes in Ingleton*
Transport	*Bus 581 to Ingleton Community Centre (closest stop) from Settle and Kirkby Lonsdale*
Parking	*Broadwood car park (LA6 3ET). Entrance fee is £10 per adult, £5 for children (under 16 years), ticket includes parking*
Toilets	*At Broadwood car park and Beezley Farm*

Time 3hr
Distance 7km (4¼ miles)
Climb 300m

A circular walk through superb oak woodland, passing spectacular waterfalls

This circular walk explores the waterfalls, woodlands and limestone scenery above Ingleton, and is well worth the entrance fee. Try to choose a clear day after rainfall when the waterfalls will be spectacular and the far-reaching views can be fully appreciated. It is a surprisingly strenuous walk with many flights of stone and wooden steps. The path is well defined and signed, but sections can be slippery and very uneven, so wear shoes with a good grip. Not suitable for pushchairs or small children.

View of Ingleborough as the route starts to drop down to more waterfalls

The impressive Thornton Force

1 From the ticket office an easy riverside path leads into a deep gorge. The woodland path continues through Swilla Glen, with the River Twiss on the right, crosses Manor Bridge, then rises to reach another bridge with a good view of **Pecca Falls**. Cross the bridge and climb steep concrete steps to gain more good views of the falls, then continue to reach the next waterfall, Hollybush Spout, with a picnic area.

2 Emerging above the gorge, the trail becomes easier for a while, with views up towards Twistleton Scar. The mighty **Thornton Force** comes into view, with several bench seats well positioned for admiring the falls and view.

Thornton Force carries the River Twiss down from Kingsdale to cascade 14m over a limestone shelf into a large pool and onwards over shallow rock shelves in the riverbed.

Climb the stone steps up the bank to the left to reach the beautiful upper river valley with its multiple cascades and fell views. Follow the path as it eases to the left, with the summit of Gragareth seen ahead.

WALK 15 – INGLETON WATERFALLS TRAIL

Gragareth, at 627m, is the second highest point in Lancashire. Ingleborough (724m), the second highest peak in the Yorkshire Dales, is to the east. You will see the multiple level layers of limestone exposed on the mountainside.

> ⓘ *Waterfalls are created when streams pass over beds or layers of harder rock, often plunging several metres to a lower level. The pools below waterfalls can be quite deep.*

3 Cross the river one more time on **Ravenray Bridge** to reach a bench and open hillside. The trail now follows a track beside the fell wall, with superb views on a clear day to the south and west. Continue straight ahead through the buildings of **Twistleton Hall** and drop to the road, with Ingleborough dominating the view.

4 Cross the road and bear right. Pass just below the toilets at **Beezleys Farm** then fork left to continue on the signed trail, following the River Doe past more spectacular waterfalls. Pass the complex cascades of **Beezley Falls**.

The river passes through a deep and narrow defile of the Baxenghyll Gorge (with an optional short detour to the left for a better view). More steps and tree roots follow to reach **Snow Falls**, the final waterfall on the trail.

5 Pass through a one-direction gate and follow an easy track above the river to reach **Ingleton**. Follow signs to the village centre for shops and cafes. To return to the car park take the steep road down opposite the Co-op (Bell Horse Gate) and then right to the car park.

‒ To shorten

It is possible to turn right at Twisleton Hall on a track, then ahead along the road (Oddies Lane) directly down to Ingleton, saving 2km (30min).

Waterfalls, caves, potholes and shakeholes

The limestone of this area features many waterfalls, caves and potholes. The pools below waterfalls can be quite deep, eroded by the force of the falling water. The fells are littered with potholes and shakeholes (usually marked on maps). Shakeholes are where the underlying limestone has been weakened and dissolved, and the softer earth above has collapsed into the void. Over time, water rich in carbon dioxide dissolves the limestone, creating potholes, opening fissures and often leading to an underground network of caves – take care when passing potholes, as some are hard to see. Many of the caves in the area can be visited, including White Scar and Ingleborough caves.

USEFUL INFORMATION

Tourism bodies

Yorkshire Dales National Park
www.yorkshiredales.org.uk

Welcome to Yorkshire
www.yorkshire.com

Visit Cumbria
www.visitcumbria.com

Tourist information centres

Sedbergh
www.sedbergh.org.uk

Kirkby Lonsdale
www.kirkbylonsdale.info

Ingleton (Ingleborough Community Centre)
www.ingleton.co.uk

Travel

Western Dales Bus
www.westerndalesbus.co.uk

S1 Dent–Sedbergh–Kendal: Wednesday and Saturday

S5 Kendal–Kirkby Stephen–Sedbergh: Friday only

Stagecoach service 563 from Kendal serves Sedbergh, Cautley and the Fat Lamb

Also see Westmorland and Furness Council
www.westmorlandandfurness.gov.uk

Settle to Carlisle Railway
https://settle-carlisle.co.uk

Taxis

On Time Taxis Sedbergh 07917 801878

Woofs of Sedbergh 01539 620 414

Further reading

Walking in the Yorkshire Dales South and West by Dennis and Jan Kelsall (Cicerone 2022) has a selection of longer routes in the region.

The Dales Way by Terry Marsh (Cicerone 2024) covers the full Dales Way trail.

© Jonathan Williams and Lesley Williams 2025
First edition 2025
ISBN: 978 1 78631 248 8
eISBN: 978 1 78765 164 7

Printed in Singapore by KHL Printing on responsibly sourced paper.
A catalogue record for this book is available from the British Library.
All photographs are by the author unless otherwise stated.
Cover illustration of Sedbergh by Clare Crooke.

© Crown copyright and database rights 2025 OS AC0000810376

Cicerone's EU representative for GPSR compliance is Easy Access System Europe, Mustamäe tee 50, 10621 Tallinn, Estonia. Email gpsr.requests@easproject.com.

CICERONE

Cicerone Press, Juniper House, Murley Moss, Oxenholme Road,
Kendal, Cumbria, LA9 7RL

www.cicerone.co.uk

Updates to this Guide

While every effort is made to ensure the accuracy of guidebooks as they go to print, changes can occur during the lifetime of an edition. Any updates that we know of for this guide will be on the Cicerone website (www.cicerone.co.uk/1248/updates), so please check before planning your trip. We also advise that you check information about transport, accommodation and shops locally. Even rights of way can be altered over time. We are always grateful for information about any discrepancies between a guidebook and the facts on the ground, sent by email to updates@cicerone.co.uk.

Register your book: To sign up to receive free updates, special offers and GPX files where available, create a Cicerone account and register your purchase via the 'My Account' tab at www.cicerone.co.uk.